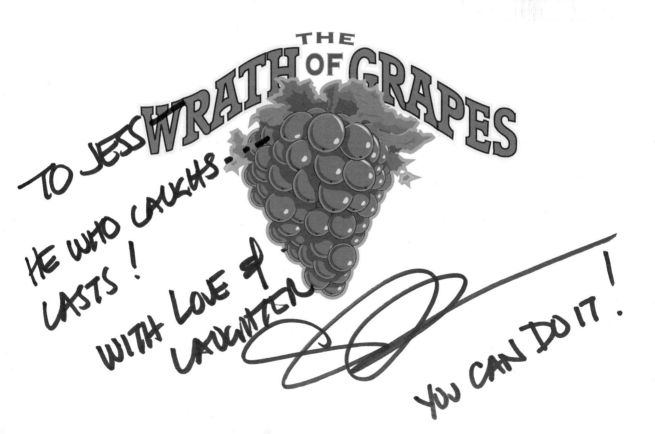

THE WRATH OF GRAPES

TO JESS

HE WHO CAUGHS...
LASTS !

WITH LOVE &
LAUGHTER

YOU CAN DO IT !

THE WRATH OF GRAPES

PACKED WITH: RECOVERY, INSIGHT, AND HUMOR

written and edited by
SANDI BACHOM

HAZELDEN®

Hazelden
Center City, Minnesota 55012-0176

1-800-328-0094
1-651-213-4590 (Fax)
www.hazelden.org

Library of Congress Cataloging-in-Publication Data
Bachom, Sandi, 1944–
   The wrath of grapes : packed with recovery, insight, and humor / written and edited by Sandi Bachom.
      p. cm.
   ISBN: 1-56838-552-8 (pbk.)
   1. Alcoholism—Miscellanea. 2. Alcoholism—Quotations, maxims, etc. 3. Recovering alcoholics—
   Miscellanea. I. Title.

HV5072 .B28 2000
362.292—dc21   00-040721
                          04 03   6 5 4 3 2

Cover design by Mark Herman
Interior design by Mark Herman
Typesetting by Universal Press

DEDICATION

To my son, Grant, my greatest gift and teacher,
and to all those who still suffer the wrath of grapes.

Definition of a hangover: The wrath of grapes.

CONTENTS

INTRODUCTION

Although it's been thirteen years since my last drink, I am no less a drunk. The passage of time does not diminish this fact. In a strange paradox, known only to alcoholics, the years actually fuel the denial that whispers to us, "I really wasn't *that* bad." This phenomenon demands that I be reminded on a daily basis that I have this affliction that is no laughing matter but that laughter can help to mend.

If we can find humor in a thing, we have already begun to heal. To discover that I was an alcoholic was not only the source of my greatest sorrow but of my greatest joy. In fact, alcohol had robbed me of my laughter.

Every word in this book has been a part of my recovery and has brought me comfort when I have been paralyzed by fear and overwhelmed with loneliness. Alcoholism is a fatal disease, but loneliness is not. If, in some small measure, I can return the gift that has been so generously given to me, then I am truly grateful.

THE WRATH OF GRAPES

A drunk finds himself wandering around a frozen lake and decides it is the perfect place to go ice fishing. With his gear in tow, he finds a likely spot and begins to saw a hole. Suddenly, a loud voice thunders from the sky, "You won't find any fish there." The drunk looks up, sees no one, and continues sawing. Again, the voice yells down, "I guess you didn't hear me. I said there's no fish there." Baffled at the disembodied voice and unable to find its source, the drunk again begins to saw. Once again, the voice booms down. "This is the last time I'm going to tell you. There are no fish here. Please leave." The drunk is paralyzed with fear and yells out, "Who are you? Are you God trying to warn me?" The voice replies, "No, I am the manager of this hockey rink."

W R A T H

When I felt the pain that I drank to avoid,
I knew it was time to stop.

First drink, with water.
Second drink, without water.
Third drink, like water.

Don't try to clear away the wreckage of the future.

Alcoholism is a progressive and fatal disease.

My best friend became my worst enemy.

Insanity is not doing the same thing over and over again expecting
different results; insanity is doing the same thing
over and over again knowing full well what the results will be!

I drank and used to feel good, then I drank and used to feel bad,
then I just drank and didn't feel at all.

Fear knocked on my door—I opened it and there was nobody there.

The heaviest thing to carry is a grudge.

Relapse starts long before the drink is drunk.

Depression is anger without the enthusiasm.

Some recovering alcoholics go through life
standing at the complaint counter.

I like to count my disasters every single day.

Alcoholics have very high pain thresholds and very low fear thresholds.

Alcohol is patient; it will wait forever for us to return to it.

Being an alcoholic does not give me the excuse to act alcoholically.

Taking the first drink is a result of poor mental attitude.

If you're not a lion tamer, don't go into the lion's den.

I collect resentments the way other people collect fine pottery.

From the bottom of the well, you can see the stars more clearly.

Defiance is the outstanding characteristic of an alcoholic.

We are not punished for our sins but BY our sins.

One drink at a time is like committing suicide on the installment plan.

What the rest of the world calls living, alcoholics call suffering.

Regarding resentments:
let one vulture live and he will pick your bones.

My favorite drink was my NEXT drink.

If you have the disease of alcoholism,
you will do one of two things: die with it, or from it.

I can't ask my sick mind to cure my sick mind.

The people we hate teach us the most.

Alcohol robbed me of my laughter.

Alcoholics wind up in the Big House,
the Bug House, or the Ice House.

Anger is one letter short of danger.

One is too many, a thousand not enough.

Don't wrestle with pigs—you both get dirty and the pig likes it.

If I could drink socially I'd get drunk every night.

DENIAL: Don't Even Notice I Am Lying

Sometimes too much drink is not enough.

Fear is faith turned inside out.

Once you have to start making rules about drinking, you know you have a problem.

The longer we think about the bad stuff, the greater is its power to harm us.

I was like a bank—you'd better get to me before 3 P.M.

To an alcoholic, having one drink is like
falling off a roof expecting to fall just one floor.

You've got a killer disease and you can't put that hearse in reverse.

I didn't have a drinking problem, I had a stopping problem.

I was a veteran of many foreign bottles.

I used to say I was dying for a drink . . . and I was.

One tequila, two tequila, three tequila . . . floor.

Regarding the first drink: When you get run over by a train, which kills you, the locomotive or the caboose?

When something good happens to me, I am sure it's going to end. When something bad happens, I know it will never end.

Alcoholism is a disease of entitlement.

Of course I can drive; I'm too drunk to walk.

Keeping resentments is like holding yourself for ransom.

I didn't drink because I had problems, I drank to get over them.

Living begins on the far side of despair.

When telling our stories, how many ways can we say,
"I fell into the Christmas tree?"

Some of us are sicker than others.

We're all here 'cause we're not all there.

We suffer for our suffering.

Expectations are resentments under construction.

Alcoholism is an equal opportunity destroyer.

Alcohol gave me wings to fly then took away the sky.

The best remedy for anger is delay.

A bad conscience has a really good memory.

Bacchus: a convenient deity invented by the ancients as an excuse for getting drunk.

Lead me not into temptation. I can find it myself.

The church is near but the road is icy;
the bar is far away but I'll walk carefully.

People who study revenge keep their own wounds green,
which otherwise would heal and do well.

A pessimist is someone who complains
about the noise when opportunity knocks.

Alcohol allowed me to act irresponsibly and
irrationally with great confidence.

Alcohol has taken more good from me than I have taken from it.

If I weren't an alcoholic, I'd drink every day!

True forgiveness does not bury the hatchet
while allowing the handle to remain exposed.

If you are patient in one moment of anger,
you will escape a hundred days of sorrow.

God has a way of compensating for weaknesses,
which is why drunks have big mouths.

The truth shall make you free, but first it shall make you angry.

Some people, when they hit rock bottom, will climb out.
When alcoholics hit rock bottom, they will begin to dig.

WARNING: Consumption of alcohol may lead you to believe that
ex-lovers are really dying for you to telephone them at four in the morning.

I envy people who drink—at least
they know what to blame everything on.

If the headache would only precede the drunk,
alcoholism would be a virtue.

Always do sober what you said you'd do drunk.
That will teach you to keep your mouth shut.

The harder you fall, the higher you bounce.

A fear faced is a fear erased.

The heart gets hard long before the liver.

Negative thoughts provide negative results.

The drink comes at the end of the slip.

After I got sober, I learned that living alone and
having a closet full of empty bottles may be a little strange!

If you don't want what we have, go back out to what you had.

Hungry, angry, lonely, tired leads to the first drink.

Reactions to life result from two basic feelings: fear or love.

If I'm really angry, I'm in fear.

I've always handled failure very well;
it's the good stuff I have trouble with.

If I think, I won't drink. If I drink, I can't think.

Hatred destroys the hater, not the hated.

I'm always waiting for the other shoe to drop.

If you feel guilty, you probably are.

I drank too much, too often, and too long.

There's a fine line between carrying the message
and spreading the disease.

We shout our weaknesses.

I am willing to make the mistakes
if someone else is willing to learn from them.

Becoming aware of my character defects
leads me to the next step: blaming my parents.

Hate is spiritual suicide.

Only some of us learn by other people's mistakes.
The rest of us have to be the other people.

What doesn't kill us, makes us stronger.

I assume full responsibility for my actions—except
the ones that are someone else's fault.

I have the power to channel my imagination into an
ever-soaring level of suspicion and paranoia.

Never talk to drunks about their drinking while they're drunk.
You're just talking to the bottle anyway.

Fear alone won't keep me sober, but it's not a bad place to start.

What the sober person has in her heart,
the drunken person has on her lips.

Alcoholism is an allergy of the body and an obsession of the mind.

The longer we dwell on our troubles, the greater is their power to harm us.

I could always make things happen, I just couldn't make them work.

I have cut my own throat with my sharp tongue.

So many character defects, so little time.

When I awake in the morning,
I scan the horizon for things to worry about.

I don't want the morning after the night before.

Mirth diffuses rage.

Pain is our teacher.

Fear is the single strongest motivating force in our lives;
the more frightened you become,
the better your chances of achieving success.

Addiction is a craving that cannot be satisfied.

When you have a dispute with someone, remember
it takes forty-two muscles to frown, whereas it only takes four muscles
to extend your right arm and smack them.

Don't beat yourself up, the world will do a good enough job without your help.

Don't lie on purpose.

Projection is living in the wreckage of the future.

You don't do drugs, they do you.

I thought there was nothing unusual in always drinking
or always searching for one.

You can't NOT believe in a God you're mad at!

When alcoholics are frightened, they attack.

Alcoholics are restless, irritable, and discontented most of the time.

When it seems that the world is against you,
maybe you're really against the world.

Fear is the great motivator at bringing out my character defects.

Loneliness knows no person like an alcoholic.

Every suggestion I don't take, I pay for.

Being an alcoholic is like being in a box with the
instructions to get out on the outside.

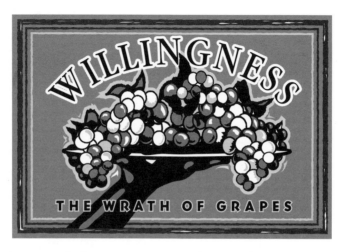

WILLINGNESS

THE WRATH OF GRAPES

A woman is on a train in a remote area and sees a sign. "Passengers without tickets will be evicted." At this point a conductor passes the woman and asks her for her ticket. The woman then reaches for her shoes, removes them and her socks, but finds no ticket. She turns the pockets of her pants and jacket inside out, but finds no ticket. Finally, the conductor says, "What's that in your pocket?"

The woman reaches in and there is the ticket. The conductor asks, "But why didn't you look there first?" The woman replies, "Because, if I had looked in my pocket first and there was no ticket, I would have no hope."

WILLINGNESS

A winner is a loser who keeps trying.

If you don't know it can't be done, you can do it.

Willpower: our willingness to use a Higher Power.

We are free at the moment we wish to be.

If I'm willing to help, then I'm willing to be helped.

A smooth sea never made a skillful sailor.

The only way out is through.

Before you say *I can't,* say *I'll try.*

Listen like only the dying can.

Choice, not chance, determines destiny.

Change only happens when the pain of holding on
is greater than the fear of letting go.

Surrender is about change.

Break a bad habit by dropping it.

Be as enthusiastic about not drinking as you were about drinking.

Admitting total defeat was the beginning of my salvation.

Let us love you until you can learn to love yourself.

Knowing what you want is the first step toward getting it.

Success is going from failure to failure with great enthusiasm.

When it becomes more difficult to suffer than to change,
you will change.

If you want happiness for a lifetime, help somebody else.

If you can't find the willingness,
try to find the willingness to find the willingness.
Go back as far as you need to.

If you want to be in the present, you have to let go of the past.

I'm not always willing to do the right things,
but I'm willing to pay the consequences
of getting caught doing them wrong.

You don't have to stop drinking; you just have to have the willingness to stop.

A turtle makes progress when it sticks out its neck.

An action beats a feeling every time.

Nothing can be changed until we accept it.

If you share your pain, you cut it in half;
if you don't, you double it.

Abstinence makes the heart grow fonder.

Practice makes progress.

You don't have to quit . . . simply surrender.

If I don't let go, I lose my grip.

The mind is like a parachute,
it works better when it's open.

What we pay attention to grows.

My brain said, "More,"
but my body said, "Enough."

Trying and failing is better than trying nothing and succeeding.

Fear is like a wall that's miles high and stretches out for
hundreds of miles in each direction but is only paper thin.
All you need to do is step through it.

Willingness is doing what I have to, whether I want to or not.

The beginning is the most important part of the work.

Surrender: I can't handle it. God, you take it.

When I accept myself, I change.
When I accept others as they are, they change.

Nothing annoys your enemies more than forgiving them.

We hit bottom when we are totally afraid.

Willpower tells me I must, but willingness tells me I can.

Patience takes patience.

Take what you can use and leave the rest.

You don't have to drink today.

When you are in pain, write a gratitude list.
Go through the alphabet assigning something to every letter.

The root of tolerance is *tolere,* which means to "give permission."

Unless I accept my virtues, I will be overwhelmed by my faults.

Serenity is not freedom from the storm, but peace amid the storm.

Have reverence for synchronicity.

Ask yourself, "What am I supposed to be learning from this?"

Success comes not by trying harder but by trying longer.

Embracing your disappointments will help you to heal faster.

Optimism is an intellectual choice.

Ask for help.

Change what you can, and change your mind about what you can't.

Forgiveness is relinquishing the role of being the victim.

It isn't about self-improvement, it's about self-acceptance.

I need to get comfortable staying stopped.

If you want to stop drinking, you can.

To an alcoholic, saying you're cutting down is admitting you have a problem.

If you're willing to do the work,
ANYTHING is possible.

HUMILITY
THE WRATH OF GRAPES
PRODUCT OF HAZELDEN

God answers prayers in three ways:
Yes, I thought you would never ask.
Yes, but not yet.
No, because I love you too much.

HUMILITY

My marriage ended exactly when it was supposed to.
But if I had known there was an expiration date,
I would have made other plans.

Doubt anything but yourself.

Alcoholics know they are making progress
when they start having illusions of adequacy.

My biggest character defect is self-pity.

Swallowing your pride rarely leads to indigestion.

If you want to see what you're giving, look at what you're getting.

I'm really a very persuasive person,
I can convince myself of anything.

Humility is that which reduces you to your
proper size without degrading you.

To dream of the person you would like to be is to waste the person you are.

Serenity is acceptance of my problem.

A pat on the back is a hug in passing.

You make a living by what you get,
and you make a life by what you give.

Three words you don't want to hear an alcoholic say:
"I've been thinking."

A person who is proud of his intelligence
is like a prisoner proud of his cell.

I was given the gift of desperation.

Self-will imprisoned me far more than bars ever did.

I'm not what I should be;
I'm not what I could be;
but I'm not what I was.

Everything I need is provided in the present.

Gratitude + Service = Humility

If you want to find humility, do something humiliating.

Love wasn't put in our hearts to stay;
love isn't love until you give it away.

Hearing is a gift. Listening, an art.

Anything that needs to be healed will usually
keep coming up in your character defects.

All you can take with you is that which you've given away.

Forgiveness is a gift of high value, yet it costs nothing.

When we stop drinking, it's not the end of our lives, it's the beginning.

The quality of my laughter has changed.
When I drank I was laughing at others, but in sobriety I laugh at myself.

Do not search for happiness; instead, search for right living.
Then happiness will be your reward.

True happiness is the result of acceptance and gratitude.

I base my self-esteem not on what others think of me,
but what I think they think of me.

Sobriety gave me a new pair of glasses.

It's easier to put on slippers than to carpet the whole world.

I once heard an old-timer say, "If anything would make me drink again,
it would be *big-shotism*."

People are unreasonable, illogical, and self-centered. Love them anyway.

Recipe for unhappiness: Find a chair, sit in a corner,
and think about yourself for twenty minutes a day.

When you're wrong, promptly admit it. Don't wait thirty years.

The center of the universe is a very crowded place.

I was terminally unique.

Ask an alcoholic what time it is and she will tell you how to build a clock.

Sometimes we must fall down before we can stand up.

The reason you pray on your knees is to give you humility.

Simply learn your lines and show up.

A recovering friend, when asked about his good fortune, said,
"Sometimes I think God's got the wrong guy!"

Alcohol preserves most things; dignity isn't one of them.

He who forgives ends the quarrel.

Bend your knees before you bend your elbow.

I am unique, just like everybody else.

Accept that some days you're the pigeon and some days you're the statue.

A good time to keep your mouth shut is when you're in deep water.

She who is sorry for having sinned is almost innocent.

No one is listening . . . until you make a mistake.

Your sole purpose in life may be
simply to serve as a warning to others.

Thank goodness for our mistakes;
they give us something to laugh about later.

It's not the load that breaks you . . . it's the way you carry it.

I always think I'm too much or not enough.

If it's your way, it's not His will.

I love you and that's my business;
I do not need your permission.

Learn to listen. Then, listen to learn.

If you don't like what people are saying about you,
maybe you should stop doing the things they are talking about.

No one has more humility than me.

If drinking doesn't bring you to your knees, sobriety will.

Assume the best.

The smallest package in the world is an alcoholic all wrapped up in himself.

Humility is truth.

Learning to love yourself is the definition of courage.

Identify, don't compare.

When you treat me special, I feel average.
When you treat me average, I feel rejected.

Forgiveness ends the war.

The path to humility is in deeds, not words.

We must forgive our enemies because
we need others more than we need pride.

None of us came here on a winning streak.

Look up to God. Look in to yourself.
Look out to others.

I didn't cause it.
I can't control it.
I can't cure it.

Everyone has the need for forgiveness.

Get it. Give it. Grow in it.

Definition of false pride:
lying in the gutter looking down on the rest of the world.

Principles before personalities.

With humility comes wisdom.

Take care of yourself first.

Do you want to be right, or do you want to be happy?

Humility is the willingness to learn.

Alcoholism is a disease of self-obsession.

The gratifying part of my recovery
is the pride I take in my humility.

Regarding humility, if you can describe it, you don't have it.

Don't drink and help another alcoholic.

The two most difficult words in the English language:
I'm sorry.

A man is stranded in his house during a hurricane. He hears a loud knock on the door, "Come on, get in the truck and we will take you to safety." "No," says the man. "All my life, I have been a God-fearing man and I have faith that He will save me." As the water rises, a boat comes by and beckons the man to get in. He declines. At last, the man is on the roof; his whole house is under water. A helicopter hovers over him, beckoning him to come aboard. He declines a third time. The water washes the man away and he drowns. When the man appears before God in heaven he cries, "I don't understand. I prayed to you my whole life and always believed you would deliver me. Why did you forsake me?" God spoke, "What do you want from me? I sent you a truck, a boat, and a helicopter!"

W I S D O M

The measure of love is how we are changed by it.

Decisions aren't forever.

If I could take away the pain . . . I wouldn't.

Whether you think you can or you think you can't . . . you're right.

There are two days a week you should never worry about:
yesterday and tomorrow.

Everything I need is provided,
and everything I want I have to work for.

Enjoy life. There's plenty of time to be dead.

Willingness without action is fantasy.

The only requirement for serenity is a desire to stop thinking.

Sometimes we have difficult times in a wonderful life.

Life is a series of comebacks.

The worst things that happen to me always turn out to be the best.

Today I have a choice.

Things turn out the best for those who
make the best of the way things turn out.

We are human beings, not human doings.

Everything that happens to you is your teacher.

Who would have thought that the worst catastrophe,
my alcoholism, would become the source of my greatest joy and laughter?

It's not what happens; it's how we interpret what happens.

When all else fails, follow the directions.

Life is a mirror. If someone irritates you,
maybe you should take a look at yourself.

If you don't learn the lesson from the experience,
you will have to re-experience the lesson.

Relationships don't end; they merely change.

The less you say the more others remember.

This too shall pass.

If you wonder about your sanity, you are sane.

If you treat a person as she is, she will remain as she is.
If you treat her for what she could be, she will become what she could be.

All that we are is the result of what we have thought.

If you keep falling in the same hole,
go down a different road.

Wisdom has two parts:
having a lot to say,
and not saying it.

There are no mistakes—only events from which we need to learn.

If you think you're happy, you are.
If you think you're wise, you are not.

Why is it we can't forget our troubles the way we forget our blessings?

The toughest problem in arithmetic
is to learn to count your blessings.

Life is a mystery to be lived,
not a problem to be solved.

Today is the tomorrow I worried about yesterday.

If you think sobriety is too simple, go out and drink some more.
By the time you get back you'll be simple enough for sobriety.

If it doesn't concern me, it doesn't concern me.

My greatest change comes after my greatest pain.

I am the sum of all the choices I have made in my life.

To understand all is to fear all.

Fear not that your life shall come to an end,
but rather that it shall never have a beginning.

When you find an alcoholic lying in the gutter, pick him up.
When you see him there again, pick him up again.
One day you will see that he is carrying you.

Marriage is less about what we have in common
and more about having humor about what we do not.

Each disappointment is part of the success.

A bend in the road is not the end of the road . . . unless you fail to make the turn.

Regarding bad things happening to good people:
First of all, things aren't that bad . . . and you aren't as good as you think.

Everything in my life that is good is because I am sober.
Everything that is bad is not, it's just life.

What's the difference between an alcoholic and a six-week-old puppy?
After a while the puppy quits whining.

Thinking about yourself will always lead to unhappiness.

Alcoholism is the most democratic disease on earth.

It takes what it takes.

As alcoholics, our windshields get dirty on the inside.

Be grateful for the gifts that come to you disguised as hardships.

Reasons to drink: self-pity, loneliness, and fear.

The value of the lesson that we need to learn
is measured by the intensity of the pain we are experiencing.

I encourage you to make mistakes; it is how we learn.

HONESTY

THE
WRATH
OF GRAPES

HAZELDEN

An alcoholic is walking along the beach when she sees a bottle. She stops and rubs it, and a genie pops out. "You have three wishes," says the genie. The alcoholic says, "I'll take a bottle that can never be emptied." Whamo! She has a bottle that can never be emptied, and she starts to drink. The genie taps her on the shoulder and says, "And what are your other two wishes?" "Oh," says the alcoholic, "I'll have two more like this one."

H O N E S T Y

If I'm not aware of my character defects, they don't count.

If you really want to stay sober, you will find a way.
If not, you will find an excuse to drink.

You'll probably get more truth out of a person who is drunk than one who is sober.

Don't romance the drink.

Relationships will do to you what alcohol didn't.

We lie loudest when we lie to ourselves.

What you do not want done to yourself, do not do to others.

Alcoholism is not in the bottle, it's in the person.

If you don't hear what you need to hear,
say what you need to hear.

The only requirement for a slip is when the desire
to drink is stronger than the desire not to drink.

She's going to get me drinking before I get her sober.

It's not my feelings that will kill me,
it's my judgments of my feelings that will kill me.

I don't like to mess with someone else's bottom.

We didn't get here by eating too damn much ice cream.

I am the architect of my own misery.

SLIP: Sobriety Loses Its Priority

Clean up your side of the street.

Alcoholism is the only disease that tells you you're all right.

If you stay sober and you don't change, you will drink.

The worst things that have happened to me have turned out to be the best, and the worst of the worst was discovering I was an alcoholic.

Another word for my alcoholic attitudes: *alcotudes*.

A drug is a drug.

I will lose anything I put before my sobriety.

Everything is exactly the way it is supposed to be right now.

I thought alcohol was the source of my laughter,
but it was the source of my pain.

I always look for the hardest way to do the easiest thing.

Cut yourself a little more slack.

Reality is for people who can't handle drugs.

YET: You're Eligible Too

I'm as dishonest today as I can live with.

LOVE: Love Openly, Validate Equally

Your beliefs create your reality.

It's all about the choices we make; it's up to us.

It wasn't my drinking, it was my thinking.

Ninety percent of your fears never come to pass . . . so stop worrying.

The dictionary is the only place where success comes before work.

Before engaging mouth, put mind in gear.

I can't be honest and take care of
your feelings at the same time.

The truth shall set you free, but first it will hurt like hell.

Better to sleep with a sober cannibal
than a drunken minister.

If you don't talk about it, you'll drink about it.

My idea of cutting back was less seltzer.

We suffer from alcohol*ism*, not alcohol*wasm*.

When you drink, you lose the right to be right.

If you don't want to slip, stay out of slippery places.

Almost everything I know about myself is wrong.

Are you *listening* or waiting to talk?

We are judged by our actions,
not our intentions.

When we admit to another the exact nature of our wrongs,
it is most likely the first time we have ever spoken them out loud.

To thine own self be true.

There is no right way to do the wrong thing.

Any degree of comfort requires rigorous honesty.

Not everything that is faced can be changed,
but nothing can be changed until it is faced.

I am not in control, but I am responsible.

As an alcoholic, my pleasure meter is broken;
I don't know when I've had enough.

My greatest problem is not my problem,
but what I think about my problem.

When you challenge an addiction,
you choose to become a whole person.

As alcoholics we have built-in forgetters.

The one person you must forgive is the one you can't.

A day at a time, more will be revealed and more will be required.

I have to learn to leave my best thinking out of most of my life.

Do you want to fix your old life? Or, do you want a new one?

Getting sober is like being in the Mafia;
once you're in you can never get out.

Don't ask, "How is the world treating me today?"
Instead, ask, "How am I treating the world today?"

Alcoholics have their arms wrapped around the bottle.
Codependents have their arms wrapped around the alcoholic.

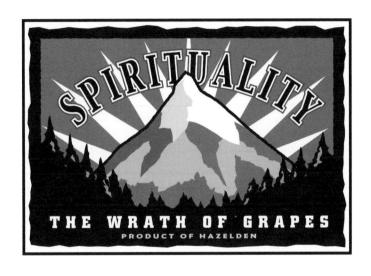

Bob is rowing in a boat with God steering next to him.
One day Bob says to God, "God, I'm getting tired of rowing,
do you mind if I steer for a while?" To which God replies,
"That would be great, Bob, but there's only one thing. I don't know how to row."

S P I R I T U A L I T Y

God gives us what we need to be healed by taking something away.

If you're having difficulty with the concept of a Higher Power,
who was driving when you were in a blackout?

It's not what you see that's real, it's what you don't see.

Religion is when we talk about God. Spirituality is when we talk with God.

God will heal your broken heart, if you will give Him all the pieces.

Faith is not belief without proof, but trust without reservation.

Let your heart guide you. It whispers, so listen closely.

God and I don't share the same watch.

If you can't do anything about it, you know it's God's will.

Don't drive faster than your guardian angel can fly.

Spirituality is where the incorrigible rely on
the invisible and achieve the impossible.

People who don't know God's will for them
are not in the habit of praying for it.

If God was small enough to be understood,
He wouldn't be big enough to be God.

Faith is daring the soul to go beyond what the eyes can see.

Believe in miracles but don't depend on them.

All I know for sure is,
I have a Higher Power and it ain't me.

I'm not the one who can keep me sober.

Please be patient. God isn't finished with you yet.

Humans can tell how many seeds are in the apple,
but only God can tell how many apples are in the seeds.

If I gain the whole world but lose my soul, what have I gained?

On final judgment day,
do you want what you deserve or do you want a forgiving God?

God looks beyond our faults to see our needs.

Give God permission.

There is only one lesson, and that is the lesson of faith.

I don't always know what God's will is for me, but I always know what it's not.

What humans can conceive, God can achieve.

My prayers used to be foxhole prayers: "God, if you get me out of this . . ."

I'd rather live my life as if there is a God and die to find out there isn't,
than to live my life as if there is no God and die to find out there is.

God got me sober and sobriety got me to God.

We don't ask God "Why?" about the gifts we are given,
but we do ask God "Why?" about the adversities.

God's will is doing the opposite of what my head tells me to do.

Higher Power, I am willing to be relieved of the need to be unworthy.
I am worthy of the very best in life,
and I lovingly allow myself to realize it now.

I'll see it when I believe it.

The moment we get sober is God's gift to us; what we do with it is our gift to God.

We are all given a moment of grace—it is the greatest gift we can receive.

Don't worry. Pray.

God helps those who don't help God too much.

Faith chases away fear.

An atheist is someone who has no invisible means of support.

I can't. God can. Let Him.

Meditate one minute a day. It will transform your life.

Sometimes just keeping my mouth shut
can be a spiritual experience.

The only thing between God and me, is me.

If you pray, why worry? If you worry, why pray?

If you have trouble praying on your knees,
put your shoes a little farther under your bed before going to sleep.

If you wonder if you are doing God's will, you are.

Sometimes the only thing between an alcoholic and a drink is his Higher Power.

Seven days without praying makes one weak.

When I see a penny on the street, I always think, "In God we trust."

Believe in God; it's easier than coming up with bail money.

If we are miserable, chances are we are not doing God's will.

Sometimes you have to get on your knees to rise.

If you don't have a Higher Power, borrow mine.

A hunch is God trying to tell you something.

Stop thinking about the problem and think about God instead.

Faith is a muscle; the more you exercise it, the stronger it gets.

The power behind me is greater than the problem in front of me.

We are not human beings sharing a spiritual journey,
but spiritual beings sharing a human journey.

Alcoholism is a low-grade spiritual search.

If you can explain it, God didn't do it.

If you can't sleep at night, don't count sheep, talk to the Shepherd.

The purpose of life is to live in a manner that invites God's love.

What we give love to we empower.

There are really only two choices: worry or trust God.

Pray daily. God is easier to talk to than most people.

Hope is a four-letter word.

When we look at life from the top of the mountain there are no limitations.

The will of God will never take you to
where the grace of God will not protect you.

God even speaks to me through people I dislike.

Don't tell God how big your problem is.
Tell your problem how big your God is.

Please Lord, teach us to laugh again,
but don't ever let us forget that we cried.

Alcohol is a chemical solution to a spiritual problem.

We are without a defense against the first drink.
Our defense must come from a power greater than ourselves.

When we listen, God speaks. When we obey, God works.

God wants for me what I would want for myself, *if* I had all the facts!

I was a hopeless dope addict . . . now I am a dopeless hope addict.

The answer is: GOD. Now, what was the question?

Stop worrying about your difficulties
and think about God instead.

Time spent laughing is time spent with God.

Healing an addiction is our deepest spiritual work.

Spirituality is the ability to get your mind off yourself.

There are no coincidences in sobriety.

When love is present, miracles are possible.

You don't have to do it alone.

If we were born living up to our full potential,
it would not be as much fun for God.

The times I really get in trouble are when I lose touch with my Higher Power.

Pray for the obsession to be lifted.

The last year of my drinking,
a power greater than alcohol was trying to get my attention.

I know God doesn't give me anything I can't handle.
I just wish He didn't have such a high opinion of me.

When you stop praying, you start planning.

Miracles happen if we allow them to.

If you're having problems with God, don't worry,
He's not having problems with you.

If you pray and don't get what you ask for,
it doesn't mean that prayers don't work. It just means the answer was "no."

If you no longer feel close to God, who moved?

God loves it when you call Him by name.

Take all the action that is within your power to take and then let go of it.
The rest is in God's hands anyway.

Hope is what is left after you lose everything.

Miracles are possible, even without our consent.

A miracle is a change in perception.

Is it odd? Or, is it God?

Relieve me of the bondage of self that I may better do Thy will.

I'm only one God away from my next drink.

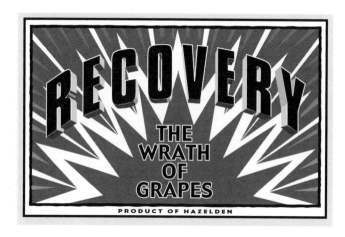

RECOVERY

THE WRATH OF GRAPES

PRODUCT OF HAZELDEN

An alcoholic walks into a bar and asks the bartender, "Did I spend $200 in here last night?" The bartender says, "Yes." "Thank God," says the alcoholic, "I thought I lost it!"

Love brings out anything unlike itself that needs to be healed.

"I" got drunk. "We" got sober.

The most important word in recovery is *We*.

Change is a process, not an event.

Recovery isn't about feelings, it's about doings.

Only an open mind can be healed.

If you live on the edge of recovery, you might fall off.

You can't speed up your recovery, but you sure can slow it down.

An ounce of prevention is worth a gallon of relapse.

I grow at the speed of pain.

If you can laugh at it then you can laugh with it.

Today I soak up sobriety the way I used to soak up alcohol.

I was waiting for my dreams to come true
until somebody suggested that maybe my dreams were waiting for *me* to come true.

A dry drunk is deprived of a drink on a daily basis;
a sober alcoholic is relieved of a drink on a daily basis.

I needed to talk to others to get sober,
and now I need to talk to others to learn how to live.

The good news about sobriety is you get to feel your feelings;
the bad news about sobriety is you get to feel your feelings.

Every disappointment is part of the success.

There are no strangers, only alcoholics I haven't met yet.

I was powerless over alcohol and my life had become unimaginable.

Recovery is not a death sentence, it's a life sentence.

Addiction is about getting out of yourself,
and recovery is about accepting yourself exactly the way you are.

First it got better, then it got worse, then it got real, then it got good.

I didn't make it all the way to the beach to drown in the sand.

Attitude creates reality.

You can stop the engine on the boat,
but the boat keeps on going for a while.

One thing you don't hear when you get sober: keep it complicated.

Regarding making amends to people who have passed away:
mail a letter to where they are buried with no return address.

If you can make yourself sick, why can't you make yourself well?

I was looking in the bottom of a bottle for
everything I have in my life right now.

Think the drink through.

Every drink I drank got me here. Every drink I don't drink keeps me here.

I didn't get sober to be miserable.

Addiction is the disease; alcohol is merely the symptom.

You're ready to get sober when you see that living in the cure
is less fearful than living in the illness.

You can't think your way into a new way of living . . .
you have to live your way into a new way of thinking.

We get sober for our drinking.
We stay sober for our thinking.

SOBER: Staying Off Booze Equals Recovery

Thank God we're not all sick at the same time.

Sobriety is like old soda bottles: no deposit, no return.

Any adversity or problem that comes to you might
be an indicator of something that needs to be healed.

Deciding to get sober is the most important decision you will ever make.

There is life after alcohol.

Sometimes I am asked, "How does sobriety work?"
I answer, "Just fine thank you."

If you want someone to stop drinking,
pray for his or her bottom to be raised.

It's the first drink that gets you drunk.

Sobriety is a club with the highest dues in the world.

Now, I only dread one day at a time.

To change and to change for the better are two different things.

We need to experience what we are experiencing in order to learn.

My life started when I stopped.

Uncover, discover, discard.

Feel, heal, deal.

I've learned to dodge the bowling balls but I still get hit by the marbles.

Change is mandatory, progress is optional.

The secret to long-term sobriety: Don't drink. Don't die.

One more drink and I might not have made it here.
One less drink and I might not have made it here.

I thought there was an easier, softer way.

Your emotional age: The age you were when you started drinking
plus the years you have been sober.

Laughter is the sound effect of recovery.

Happiness is merely the remission of pain.

Our guarantee: You will not drink while
carrying the message to a still-suffering alcoholic.

Every mistake I have ever made has helped me grow.

When the pain of staying sober becomes less than the pain of getting drunk,
you'll stay sober.

Sobriety makes me into who God wanted me to be all along.

Half measures availed us nothing.

Keep company with those who make you better.

There is pain in recovery, but misery is optional.

Addiction is pain plus learned relief.

I heal by listening to you tell your story.

If you don't go through the pain
you will never learn the lesson you were supposed to.

All healing is essentially the release from fear.

Change is uncomfortable.

The quest for sanity is the most insane thing I have ever done.

When one forgives completely, the space is immediately filled with love.

The pain is the most severe in the area that needs to be healed.

All paths of healing go through forgiveness and love.

All the work is about accountability or acceptance.

Sobriety is a process of recovering who we are.

If you have no tools for living, I'll lend you mine.

If you don't take the first drink, you won't get drunk.

Hope is the first step toward recovery.

Service is the antidote for fear.

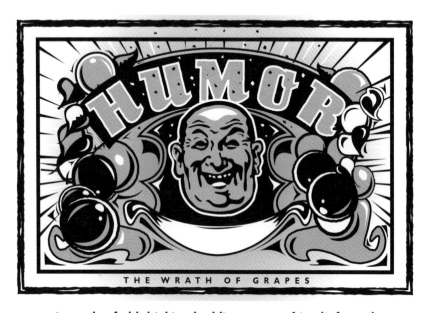

HUMOR

THE WRATH OF GRAPES

A couple of old drinking buddies are at a friend's funeral.
As they pass by the open casket, one remarks, "Jane looks
surprisingly good." "She should," retorts her friend.
"She hasn't had a drink in three days!"

H U M O R

Of all the things I lost as a result of my alcoholism,
I miss my mind the most!

Drinking has gotten me two things in life: fat and broke.

Laughter is the cheapest and most effective pain reliever.

Trying to get sober alone is much like leaving
Dracula in charge of the blood bank.

I have to ask myself,
"What would an adult do in this situation?"

Laughter is the shortest distance between two people.

I only got drunk once . . . but it lasted for twenty-five years.

If you want to hide something from an alcoholic,
put it in a Bible.

Alcoholism is the only disease I know that when the treatment fails,
we blame the patient.

Nonalcoholic beer is for nonalcoholics.

Thank you, God, for the beautiful day I'm going to have
if I can just get rid of my attitude.

When a nonalcoholic gets a flat tire, she calls AAA.
When an alcoholic gets a flat tire,
she calls suicide prevention.

Before you criticize someone, you should walk a mile in his shoes.
That way when he figures out what happened,
you will be a mile away from him, *and* you will have his shoes.

How can you tell if an alcoholic is lying? Her lips are moving.

Find humor in a thing and you can survive it.

Only to another drunk can you make the most horrible admissions
and make that person laugh.

If my brain didn't need me for transportation,
it would have killed me a long time ago.

I was amazed at how good orange juice tasted without the vodka.

If a fly lands in the beer of a normal drinker,
he will order a new beer.
If a fly lands in the beer of a problem drinker,
he will shoo away the fly and drink the beer.
If a fly lands in the beer of an alcoholic,
he will pick up the fly, shake it, and shout, "Spit it out, spit it out!"

Yeah, I guess I used to suppress my feelings.
Every time someone asked, "How ya doin'?" I'd reply,
"I'll get back to you as soon as I find out."

I didn't experiment with alcohol and drugs.
I was in advanced research and development.

Why is it when I talk to God I'm praying,
but when God talks to me I'm schizophrenic?

I am grateful I have been given two ears and only one mouth.

God grant me patience . . . right now.

I have to be dragged kicking and screaming into bliss.

I am afflicted with a lot of happiness.

Why should I waste my time reliving the past
when I can spend it worrying about the future?

If an alcoholic is offered the choice between the whole world and a drink,
she will invariably say, "I'll get back to you on that."

I had a near-life experience with alcohol for twenty-five years.

This is probably as bad as it can get . . . but don't count on it.

I'll have what the guy on the floor is having.

Joy is deeper than sorrow.

It's okay to take someone else's inventory;
at least you'll be thinking about someone else.

Every time we laugh we take a kink out of the chain of life.

Humor is a way of maintaining acceptance.

Denial is like sticking your head in the sand.
If your head is in the sand, what part of you is sticking up and vulnerable?

Humor at the right moment can rescue us
from taking ourselves too seriously.

You can tell a person's character by what they laugh at.

I was allergic to alcohol. I used to break out in spots:
London, New York, Los Angeles.

Did you hear about the guy who stopped drinking?
Actually, he's still drinking but under an assumed name.

I try to take one day at a time,
but lately several days have attacked me at once.

Life is like wrestling a gorilla. You don't stop when you get tired,
you stop when the gorilla gets tired.

How many codependents does it take to screw in a lightbulb?
None, they detach from it and let it screw itself.

I still have the voices in my head, but now I listen to them one at a time.

An alcoholic will wake up with her house on fire
and go looking for the matches.

I'm not getting into this lifeboat until I know why the ship is sinking!

Definition of an alcoholic:
Someone you don't like who drinks as much as you do.

The only wish that will ever be granted starts with, "I'd rather die than . . ."

The neighborhood between your ears is a very dangerous place.

Go ahead, take my inventory, everyone else does.

There are enough drunks in the world;
they certainly won't miss me.

When we share common experiences and pain, we laugh.
We heal in our common ground.

Irritated wife: "What do you mean by coming home half drunk?"
Alcoholic husband: "It's not my fault. . . . I ran out of money."

How can you tell when two alcoholics are on their second date?
There's a moving van in the driveway.

She who does not remember the past is
condemned to forget where she parks her car.

When I drank I thought others were more interesting.

I was a practicing alcoholic and
I was going to keep practicing till I got it right.

You might have a drinking problem if you awaken with
an overwhelming feeling that you should go back and apologize,
but you don't remember where you were or who you insulted.

My spiritual awakening occurred when there was a
flash of light with a cop behind it.

There is a fine line between drunks and people who are just plain nuts.

If you know you're going to look back on today and laugh,
you might as well start laughing now.

Change is inevitable, except from vending machines.

As long as you can laugh at yourself you will never cease to be amused.

Nobody ever died laughing.

WARNING: Consumption of alcohol may actually *cause* pregnancy.

Procrastination is the alcoholic who vows to stop drinking
but never gets around to it.

I only drank when I was alone or with someone.

A clear conscience is usually the sign of a bad memory.

A conscience is what hurts when all your other parts feel so good.

You can tell you're an alcoholic
if you laugh at the stories other alcoholics tell.

Today is the last day of your life . . . so far.

WARNING: Consumption of alcohol may lead you to believe you are invisible.

When taking the drinking test, "Do you drink alone?" "Yes . . . socially."
"Do you black out?" "Yes . . . socially."

If an alcoholic says something in a forest and
there's no codependent there to hear him, is he still wrong?

They tell me I live in a dysfunctional home. That scares me because I live alone.

Drunk is feeling sophisticated when you can't say it.

It is all right to drink like a fish providing you drink what a fish drinks.

When alcoholics find themselves in a rut, they move in furniture.

The secret source of humor is not joy, but sorrow.

If the back of your head keeps getting hit by the toilet seat,
you may be an alcoholic.

If every meal you've had in the past month has required a bottle opener,
you may be an alcoholic.

There is not one shred of evidence to support the idea that life is serious.

What's the difference between a rich person who drinks too much
and a poor person who drinks too much?
The rich person is an alcoholic and the poor person is a drunkard!

Why does an alcoholic have arthritis?
Because she's always stiff in one joint or another.

If you use napkins as business cards, you might be an alcoholic.

As an alcoholic, I have a preference of fantasy over reality.

I was allergic to alcohol; when I drank,
I used to break out in handcuffs.

I no longer need to punish, deceive, or compromise myself.
Unless, of course, I want to stay employed.

A true control freak knows the expiration date
on the milk cartons in the refrigerator.

Reality is an illusion created by alcohol deficiency.

United we stand, divided we stagger.

When humor crops up, resentments slip away.

Humor is a way of maintaining acceptance.

Laughter is the body's own morphine.

A belly laugh is internal jogging.

Only the first bottle is expensive.

Definition of a blackout: all that fun for nothing.

Frogs have it easy—they can eat what bugs them.

Laughter reminds us what we have in common.

I was a periodic drinker. I drank, period.

I couldn't figure out if I was a writer with an alcoholic problem
or an alcoholic with a writing problem.

An entire decade was missing to me.

My drug of choice was usually yours.

Tonight I'm going to find out just what happens when I black out.

An alcoholic would rather read about having a relationship
than actually have one.

The only time I ever had one drink
was when I misunderstood the question.

I was inducted into the Alcohol of Fame.

If drinking is interfering with your work,
you're probably a heavy drinker.
However, if work is interfering with your drinking,
you're probably an alcoholic.

I'm not an alcoholic. I'm a social drinker with blackouts.

Saying you're an alcoholic and an addict is like
saying you're from New York, New York.

I'm at one with my duality.

I wonder how many people in denial aren't aware of it?

I was a winette—a woman who only drank white wine.

You may be an alcoholic if your doctor finds
traces of blood in your alcohol stream.

Alcoholic's To Do List:
Pick up milk
Do laundry
Finish college

My idea of a diet was white wine spritzers and NO food.

About the Author

The Wrath of Grapes is Sandi Bachom's second book. Her first is the ever popular *Denial Is Not a River in Egypt.* She lives with her son in New York City where she is director of broadcast production at Mad Dogs and Englishmen, an advertising agency. She has been in recovery for more than thirteen years.

Hazelden Information and Educational Services is a division of the Hazelden Foundation, a not-for-profit organization. Since 1949, Hazelden has been a leader in promoting the dignity and treatment of people afflicted with the disease of chemical dependency.

The mission of the foundation is to improve the quality of life for individuals, families, and communities by providing a national continuum of information, education, and recovery services that are widely accessible; to advance the field through research and training; and to improve our quality and effectiveness through continuous improvement and innovation.

Stemming from that, the mission of this division is to provide quality information and support to people wherever they may be in their personal journey—from education and early intervention, through treatment and recovery, to personal and spiritual growth.

Although our treatment programs do not necessarily use everything Hazelden publishes, our bibliotherapeutic materials support our mission and the Twelve Step philosophy upon which it is based. We encourage your comments and feedback.

The headquarters of the Hazelden Foundation are in Center City, Minnesota. Additional treatment facilities are located in Chicago, Illinois; New York, New York; Plymouth, Minnesota; St. Paul, Minnesota; and West Palm Beach, Florida. At these sites, we provide a continuum of care for men and women of all ages. Our Plymouth facility is designed specifically for youth and families.

For more information on Hazelden, please call **1-800-257-7800.** Or you may access our World Wide Web site on the Internet at **http://www.hazelden.org.**